Compassion

Published in the United States of America by Cherry Lake Publishing
Ann Arbor, Michigan
www.cherrylakepublishing.com

Reading Adviser: Marla Conn, MS, Ed., Literacy specialist, Read-Ability, Inc.
Book Designer: Jennifer Wahi
Illustrator: Jeff Bane

Photo Credits: ©MNStudio/Shutterstock, 5; ©Evgeniy Kalinovskiy/Shutterstock, 7; ©A3pfamily/
Shutterstock, 9; ©Jacob Lund/Shutterstock, 11; ©Monkey Business Images/Shutterstock, 13;
©wavebreakmedia/Shutterstock, 15, 21; ©William Perugini/Shutterstock, 17; ©Flamingo Images/
Shutterstock, 19; ©Odua Images/Shutterstock, 23; Cover, 6, 10, 16, Jeff Bane; Various vector images
throughout courtesy of Shutterstock.com

Library of Congress Cataloging-in-Publication Data has been filed and is available at catalog.loc.gov

Printed in the United States of America
Corporate Graphics

About the author: Katie Marsico is the author of more than 200 reference books for children and young adults. She lives with her husband and six children near Chicago, Illinois.

About the illustrator: Jeff Bane and his two business partners own a studio along the American River in Folsom, California, home of the 1849 Gold Rush. When Jeff's not sketching or illustrating for clients, he's either swimming or kayaking in the river to relax.

Ouch!

At times, we feel pain.

It can hurt our body.

It can hurt our feelings.

Seeing pain can make us sad.

That's okay. It shows we care!

Concern is part of **compassion**.

We don't like others to suffer.

We want them to feel better.

Sometimes that means helping them solve a problem.

It almost always means showing kindness.

We also need to be kind to ourselves.

People aren't perfect.

Yet we must learn how to find joy.

What do you like about yourself?

Being kind to ourselves helps others.

We're more **content**.

Our mind is clearer.

We're able to **focus** more on the people around us.

Picture yourself at school.

You have a new classmate.

He trips and falls.

Would you keep walking or help him up?

You'd help him up.

Compassion connects us.

What is something nice you've done?

Sometimes showing compassion takes work.

Life is busy.

Still, we must be **mindful** of feelings in this moment.

To focus, we need to relax.

That's why some people **meditate**.

It's why others do **yoga**.

Talking about feelings also helps.

Compassion has many forms.

Each involves kindness.

How can you be mindful today?

glossary

compassion (kuhm-PASH-uhn) an awareness of suffering and a desire to relieve it

concern (kuhn-SURN) worrying about something or showing you care

content (kuhn-TENT) happy in a peaceful, accepting way

focus (FOH-kuhs) to give your attention to

meditate (MED-ih-tate) to train your mind to relax and focus

mindful (MINDE-ful) aware of your body, mind, and feelings

yoga (YOH-guh) poses, breathing, and sometimes meditation and chanting that provide balance and good health

index